THE CA

The Camera Obscura is one of Hugh Scott's personal favourites among his books, "because it is such a strange tale". It is a book of chilling power, as you would expect from the Master of Menace, but there is strong emotional content too. "My books are about love," says the author. "Even the most horrible of them. They are about my hero or heroine over-coming fearful odds – not by being more terrible than the enemy, but by drawing on decent things within themselves, like courage, kindness, honesty and decency." In *The Camera Obscura,* young Spindletrim must draw on all his positive qualities to triumph over the bullies who make his life a misery.

It was in 1984, two years after winning the Woman's Realm Children's Story Writing Competition that Hugh Scott decided to give up his job as an art teacher and become a full-time writer: "I had this feeling inside me, just sitting in my solar plexus – a little diamond of pure knowledge, very hard and strong, and I knew it wouldn't go away until I left teaching and became a writer." His first novel, *The Shaman's Stone,* was published in 1988 and several more titles soon followed. These include *Why Weeps the Brogan?* (Winner of the 1989 Whitbread Children's Novel Award), *The Haunted Sand, Something Watching, The Gargoyle, A Box of Tricks, The Place Between, A Ghost Waiting, Freddie and the Enormouse,* and, most recently, *The Ghosts of Ravens Crag.*

Hugh Scott is married with two grown-up children and lives in Scotland.

Other books by the same author

A Box of Tricks
Freddie and the Enormouse
A Ghost Waiting
The Gargoyle
The Plant that Ate the World
The Shaman's Stone
Something Watching
Why Weeps the Brogan?

THE CAMERA OBSCURA

HUGH SCOTT

WALKER BOOKS

AND SUBSIDIARIES

LONDON · BOSTON · SYDNEY

First published 1990 by Walker Books Ltd
87 Vauxhall Walk, London SE11 5HJ

This edition published 1996

2 4 6 8 10 9 7 5 3 1

Printed in Great Britain

British Library Cataloguing in Publication Data
A catalogue record for this book is available
from the British Library.

ISBN 0-7445-4794-6

For Gladys

CHAPTER ONE

Oh! Feel sorry for Spindletrim as he runs from bullies in the playground.

Spindletrim Tom feels sorry for himself as his tiny legs race around children, and his ears hear William Cranston's feet beat the tarmac.

William Cranston is thick-limbed and tall as a man, and sparks leap as his feet beat, as he runs easily, after Spindletrim.

Spindletrim feels sorry for himself when fat Arnold Fetter rushes, forcing Spindletrim against a wall.

Arnold Fetter is as tall as a woman and smells of sweat even on the coldest day. His jacket is dribbled with food. His waistcoat (Arnold Fetter likes to borrow his father's waistcoat) is dribbled with food. And his shirt is dribbled with food. Spindletrim thinks Arnold Fetter's underwear is probably dribbled with food. And his skin.

Something like a stone hit Spindletrim's arm. When he snatched his arm away, something like another stone hit his ribs. But the stony things were fists, mean fists, full of bones, and attached to the fists were wrists, and all the rest of bony Robert Snarkey, who was the smallest of the three bullies, but quite the nastiest, because he practised being nasty.

Spindletrim knew he practised because he saw Robert Snarkey every school day hurting children with his fists, kicking with his steel-tipped boots, cutting them – in a way – with horrid words; and he practised – everyone knew this – in a mirror in the cloakroom, finding worse ways to sneer, more terrible scowls; sniggering and laughing so his voice could follow you from one end of the street to the other; so he could bellow from the top deck of a tram-car . . .

As the fists struck Spindletrim's ribs; as Arnold Fetter's sticky palms banged on Spindletrim's ears; as William Cranston's fingers pulled his hair, and their three voices laughed and made stupid remarks, Spindletrim wished he could stay at home instead of coming to school.

School was a worrying place for Spindletrim. He worried about being late. He worried about being early and meeting the bullies. How terrible to be bullied at quarter to nine in the morning!

He worried in class about being bullied after class. Why was it important that the Battle of Britain was in 1066? That didn't help Spindletrim to get home faster; to dash from school when the bell rang, dodging through streams of pupils; running hard in

High Street; stopping to pant behind the pillar box; racing along the pavements where shops sat bright and fat, into streets where lamp posts shone on their own feet and left little room between their iron bodies and house walls.

Then Spindletrim would thud downhill among taller and taller buildings, so that the sky got thinner between the gutters, and echoes whispered for ever; until he reached a lamp post that shared its glow with the antique shop that was home.

The shop was black with age. ANTIQUES in gold paint looked down from above the single window – or would have looked down, except that a burst gutter near the sky dropped water, wiping away the QU, staining a green line down the building, leaving the letters ANTI   ES. So Spindletrim's home was called *Auntie's*, or to less imaginative people, "that junk shop in Steep Street".

Suddenly.

In the playground, the bullies stopped bullying Spindletrim. William Cranston's thick arms barred the blows from Robert Snarkey and Arnold Fetter; and Spindletrim spent the rest of that school day worrying why William Cranston had grinned.

Spindletrim ran home; through the junk shop, down the little passage to the kitchen.

Grandfather was pouring water, boiling, into the mottled grey teapot. On the table sat a plate with pretty cracks like a spider's web, and bread on it, squelching with lemon curd.

Spindletrim gulped down a bite, then remembered the bullies, and pain throbbed in his bruises.

Tears blobbed. His jaw juddered. He wailed, wishing he wasn't wailing.

Grandfather's hand patted Spindletrim's fingers, but Grandfather's face – thin as Spindletrim's, and kind – spoke no word of comfort.

So Spindletrim sobbed until the sobs decided to stop.

He finished his bread and tea, then washed his face with cold water that dashed from the one brass tap into a sink as spider-webbed as Spindletrim's plate. He rubbed his face on a towel that eased into holes as he dried between his fingers. He reached tip-toes with the towel onto a string above the cooker, then wandered into the shop.

Spindletrim enjoyed the shop. He understood that bottles were for blowing into, and the alligator's teeth were a cage for the alligator's black tongue. The grandfather clock was a friend towering in the shop's dullest corner, waiting, with a painted smile, for time to catch up with the hands which pointed at sixty-eight minutes past midnight.

So Spindletrim blew into bottles, and twanged a banjo. He squeezed between walls of furniture, and spoke to a corn dolly so delicate that even Spindletrim's straw-thin fingers dented her grassy dress. Then shadows lurched between the street light and the window.

The door jangled, crashing open, jangled crashing shut, filling the shop with the dark bulk of William Cranston, Arnold Fetter and Robert Snarkey.

CHAPTER TWO

"'Ere!" sneered Robert Snarkey. "He! He! He! He! Heeee! Wot a load of junk!"

"Junk!" squeaked Arnold Fetter.

"Most of it's junk," said William Cranston. "This banjo f'rinstance." He shook the banjo and bumped it on its shelf, making the strings hum nervously.

Grandfather, saw Spindletrim, stood at the passage curtain. The bullies roamed the shop, taller than Grandfather, picking things up, picking at a label on a stone jam jar, brushing close to Spindletrim, making Spindletrim's heart flutter like a bug among his ribs; this was why William Cranston had grinned! He had come to bully Spindletrim *at home!*

Spindletrim wished Grandfather would do something.

A jug fell, breaking itself on the floorboards.

"Sorry!" sneered Robert Snarkey.

"Three and sixpence, please," said Grandfather's thin face. Spindletrim saw Grandfather's white hair, white and silky, slide on the worn collar of his shirt. And Spindletrim despaired, for Grandfather was smaller than the smallest bully, and thin as twigs, useless, helpless, hopeless, feeble –

12

"Three and sixpence, please." Calm.

"He! He! He! He! He!" sniggered Robert Snarkey. "Sorry, sir. Never pay for something I ain't bought! He! He! He!"

"He! He!" snorted Arnold Fetter.

"Yeah," said William Cranston. "Sorry. Sorry. Oops." Old postcards sprayed from William Cranston's fingers, flattening on the floorboards.

"Help me pick them up for the old gentleman," crowed William Cranston. The bullies bent, scrabbling for the cards, Arnold Fetter's vast bottom making Spindletrim's toes curl and the sole of his shoe slither on the floor; but Grandfather's glance stopped him.

Then the bullies left, crashing the door, shadows bobbing between the street light and the shop window, Robert Snarkey's laughter rising among the dark buildings. On the counter the cards lay crushed and torn into pieces.

"Oh, Grandad!"

"Another cup of tea," suggested Grandfather.

The cup of tea grew into a meal, but the meal was silent and Spindletrim tearful. Grandfather watched Spindletrim, thinking, it seemed, about Spindletrim, rather than about the bullies.

Then bedtime crept up, and Spindletrim climbed the staircase to his room.

Where he lay awake. Thinking he could dodge Robert Snarkey's fists, and crack the bully's nose. Thinking he would duck under Arnold Fetter's slaps and sink a kick into his dangling stomach. Thinking he would run along the wall around the playground and stamp on William Cranston's head.

He would escape, of course! by climbing among the school's windows and, balancing in gutters, splash water onto the bullies' raging faces.

Then he sat in class (in his imagination) and knew immediately that Peking was fourteen miles two-hundred and fifty-two yards from Trafalgar Square where Wellington sat on a lion. *Yes, sir, I'm quite sure it's two-hundred and fifty-two. Not two-hundred and fifty-four. Do look it up in your geography book, sir. You'll find I'm right.* Spindletrim smiled as the class applauded.

He slept.

Next day, in the playground

"'Ere!" said Robert Snarkey, scowling a medium-bad scowl at Spindletrim, punching Spindletrim teasingly on the chest, "Where does your grandad get his money? Eh? Does he sell that junk? Eh?"

"Eh?" said Arnold Fetter.

"He must have money somewhere," said

William Cranston.

"Maybe in a bottle," squeaked Arnold Fetter.

"Yeh. A bottle," sneered Robert Snarkey.

"Which bottle?" demanded William Cranston.

Oh, dear. Poor Spindletrim.

Poor Spindletrim's insides jiggled. His breath was no sooner out than it wanted in.

His cheeks felt slack, and he gritted his teeth, but his cheeks wouldn't tighten even though he thought his teeth would crumble.

He didn't want to be afraid, but his body was afraid.

Arnold Fetter's sticky slap echoed on his ear, making Spindletrim's breath slide out in a big wet sob! oh! don't cry! *don't cry!* Spindletrim squealed with rage at his weeping body, and swept aside Robert Snarkey's teasing fist and strode forward and did what he dreamed of doing! *Did it!* Sweep! went Spindletrim's little leg! Up! Hard and swift! Spindletrim's toe bit Robert Snarkey's shin, and the bully yelped and danced back.

Spindletrim fled. Under William Cranston's reaching fingers. Past Arnold Fetter's stained waistcoat. Fled among pupils, pushing at backs and arms to escape from the beat of William Cranston's feet, the clatter of Robert Snarkey's steel-tipped boots, the pounding bulk of Arnold Fetter.

Then only Arnold Fetter's feet thumped at Spindletrim's heels.

Spindletrim darted through the school gate, raced between a bus and the school wall, and something dropped in front of him and he ran into it with a muffling *bump!* and William Cranston's large hands held him. Spindletrim knew the bully had come over the wall. He jerked free and ran full fat into Arnold Fetter. Jeers struck his ears, and fists struck his head, and something steel-tipped hit his legs; voices yelled until the world grew calm, and Spindletrim's body no longer minded being kicked.

Cold water bathed his face. Something stung his arm and he disappeared.

Spindletrim woke on his own mattress with the spring that annoyed his right shoulder. He smelled the fluffy smell of his blankets, and felt the cool touch of his quilt on the tip of his nose.

He sighed, but the sigh left his head through his nostrils instead of from between his lips.

Spindletrim told his lips to open, and electric messages scattered around his cheeks, tightening muscles, but Spindletrim's lips were fat and heavy, his mouth like a fold in Arnold Fetter's stomach – and his lips lay shut.

Spindletrim asked his eyes to open, and his right eye opened but his left eye seemed stuck with lemon curd. The quilt was a cliff.

Beyond the cliff, Spindletrim's bedroom door wore green paint, cool as the bottom of a pond. Spindletrim's tartan dressing-gown hung on a hook on the door like a headless body hanging in the pond's green water.

If Spindletrim's left eye had opened, he would have seen his chest of drawers painted as cold as the door; and if his head had turned, he would have seen his spotty mirror; he would see *in* the mirror, daylight squeezing through the paper-thin curtains; he would see – if he ever sat up – the carpet, so worn, it was little more than a layer of string going this way, and another layer going that.

Grandad, thought Spindletrim. He didn't mean to think it; he meant to say it; to yell it, but his tongue lay like a stone in his mouth.

He sent his fingers to explore. But his fingers only stirred, like a spider's legs against the blanket, sending fear thrilling up his spine, making his breath rush through his nose, and tears creep from his good eye. He growled at this miserable body.

Then the tears ungummed his left eye and his mouth cracked open. Pain! exploded across his face. His voice rang around the room and invisible bullies pushed needles between his ribs, into his legs –

"Spindletrim! Grandad's coming!" The body on the door dangled as the door opened.

Grandfather's hand lifted Spindletrim's head. His other hand aimed a glass at Spindletrim's fat lips and water turned the stone into his tongue.

"Oh!" gasped Spindletrim. "Grandad!"

"Grandad's here."

"Oh!" Spindletrim's voice fled in a *hoot!* from his chest. *Hoot!* "Grandad!" *Hoot!* He couldn't help it. *Hoot!* He hated it! *Hoot! Hoot! Hoot!*

Grandad's hand pressed cool on Spindletrim's brow. The hooting softened into sobs.

Grandad held Spindletrim against the cold pattern of his watch-chain; the scent of tobacco.

He eased Spindletrim back onto the pillow. "Tea, little Spindletrim."

Kitchen sounds tip-toed up the stair, and water rattled in the pipe that slept inside the bedroom wall. Tea came on a tray, with bread and lemon curd; and the tea tasted hot and sweet, and Spindletrim's body felt alive again, though bullies still jabbed in needles; but now it didn't matter.

He sat up, breath shuddering as he sipped, as he munched; watching Grandad; Grandad watching him; eyes, blue, and kind.

And fearless.

Spindletrim paused in his sipping. His own face was not fearless. When he looked in the spotty mirror his face was tight with fear. Even when there was nothing to be afraid of.

He loathed himself.

"Why are you always afraid?" he would ask the mirror, but his reflection only ever stared, tense, and cold as glass.

But.

This *but* – had crawled into Spindletrim's life so slowly that it was a long time before he noticed it. Then he noticed it. Sitting quietly at the edge of his mind. Watching him. Like another little Spindletrim. While he cried, this new Spindletrim watched. While he was afraid, this Spindletrim watched. Two Spindletrims.

"Are there two of me, Grandad?" he asked as he sipped his tea.

He was astonished when his grandad said, "Yes," as if he understood the question.

"Really?"

"Really."

"Are there two of you?"

"No." Grandfather Tom's silver hair rustled on his collar as he turned to reach the teapot. He refilled Spindletrim's mug.

"Is it just me?"

"Everyone is two people. They talk to themselves inside their heads and never think there are two. They dream as you dream,

Spindletrim. They tell themselves what they would do if only they were bigger; or older; or prettier or cleverer. But these are dreams of moonbeams, little Spindletrim."

"Moonbeams?"

"Being stronger or cleverer is as useful as changing your coat. But changing the real Spindletrim . . ."

Grandfather took Spindletrim's mug. "Enough. Sleep now. Slide down."

"Do I have to go to school?"

"No."

The door closed and the quilt was a cliff.

Spindletrim remembered his question to Grandfather, "Are there two of you?" and the answer, "No."

Then his eyes slid shut and he slept again.

The next morning

Spindletrim woke in darkness, but the pipe in the wall gurgled and he knew Grandad was up.

Spindletrim sighed. His lips felt less like Arnold Fetter's stomach.

Spindletrim's bruised flesh was as stiff as stale bread, and walking squeezed gasps from his lungs. It took all the grit in his thin little jaw to keep his cheeks from juddering. But he creaked into his tartan dressing-gown, smiling at the Spindletrim in the mirror, smiling into tearless eyes.

The gas cooker shone. The table stood

tippy-toe on the lino and the lino pretended to be parquet, though curled at the edges and worn into holes around the cooker's feet. Dull blue curtains shut out the dawn, but kept in the cosy electric light.

Grandfather Tom helped Spindletrim up onto a chair and served bacon as crisp as an autumn day, sausage spitting fat, scrambled egg, toast and marge, and a mug of tea. Spindletrim ate so fast he was quite tired as he cruised a scrap of toast around his empty plate, soaking up egg juice.

"Ha!" sighed Grandfather Tom.

"Ha!" sighed Spindletrim. He watched Grandfather stretch past the towel on the string, to the shelf, and lift a spill from a tin printed with the king's photograph. He lit the spill at the cooker – which stayed alight to warm the kitchen – and sucked the spill's flame into his pipe, tamping down curling hot tobacco with his thumb, smoke rolling towards the light bulb. The smell of Grandfather's pipe ate up the scent of bacon.

"So," said Grandfather, and backed into his rocking-chair. He rocked, one heel on the lino, ankles crossed. "Feeling better?"

"They'll come back."

"I expect so." Grandfather didn't waste time asking "who?"

"Arnold Fetter says you have money in a bottle."

"Does he now?" Grandfather puffed.

"We could tell the police."

"If the police came, young Fetter wouldn't." Rock.

"You want the bullies to come?!" Spindletrim's stomach suddenly decided it didn't need so much breakfast. He gasped, trying not to vomit; trying not to weep.

Rock went Grandfather, and the chair made a whumping sound. Rock. Blue eyes watching.

"What is it?" gasped Spindletrim. "Grandad?"

Whump. Puffing smoke.

"There are two Spindletrims inside you."

Spindletrim forgot to feel sick.

"The Spindletrim," said Grandfather, "that doesn't want to cry, is the real Spindletrim. You must get rid of the other one." Puff.

Spindletrim frowned. "But . . ." he said. Then he thought, *I am the Spindletrim that cries. I am the Spindletrim that feels so afraid. The Spindletrim that watches is tiny; a mite on the edge of my mind.*

He said, "But . . ."

Grandfather's mouth moved around his pipe. Rock.

"But the part of me that watches is so small! The *weeping part* is me!"

Puff.

"Grandad?"

Whump.

"How can I get rid of myself?"

Grandfather's lips curved up. He removed the pipe from his face. Kind eyes. Eyes that did not say, "You're pathetic," or "You are wonderful." They simply knew all about him.

Silence grew as thick as Grandfather's pipe smoke, with the *whump* of the rocking-chair outside the silence.

Spindletrim blinked under Grandfather's stare. He pushed his fork nervously about his plate.

The whumping ceased.

"You are an honest child," murmured Grandfather. "An honest child can keep a secret."

The black pipe stem shone wet at Spindletrim. "This secret can never be told. Understand?"

Spindletrim nodded.

"Say 'yes'," commanded Grandfather.

"Yes."

"Hmn." *Whump* said the chair, as Grandfather Tom rocked out of it and stepped towards the door.

Spindletrim jumped, slippered feet slapping the lino. "Grandad?"

"Yes?"

"A secret?"

Grandfather rested one hand on the door-handle, thumbed the tobacco in his pipe until it stopped wisping. He looked at Spindletrim.

Slowly, he smiled. The smile cut creases in his cheeks. Spiders' webs gathered around his eyes. His eyes bunched into blue sparkles.

And the grey mottled teapot was suddenly the most beautiful object Spindletrim had ever seen. The gas cooker on its neat feet was the most perfect cooker in the world; and the towel on its bright line of string was a delight to Spindletrim's opened senses.

Then his glance raced back to Grandfather Tom, and the old man stood so spirited that for a moment he was young again and magnificent.

"Grandfather?" whispered Spindletrim.

"It is the beginning!" breathed Grandfather. "Come. Come, little Spindletrim!" And he vanished into the passageway.

CHAPTER THREE

Spindletrim scliffed in his slippers. The curtain flapped at the end of the passage as Grandfather stepped into the shop.

A switch clicked, dropping light on the dusty tops of furniture. Bottles wore dusty cloaks. An Arnold Fetter-of-a-bottle sat fat and unpleasant for blowing into because of its smell. Spindletrim frowned.

He remembered the day a man had brought the bottle to Grandfather, and placed it on the floor – where it still waited.

Nothing, Spindletrim realized, had been sold.

Umbrellas leaned, limp as bats in the elephant's foot. Ghosts of objects floated inside unwiped glass cases. Clocks stuck, too stiff-limbed to tell the time. Sacks of magazines slumped, like dozing people. All unsold.

Spindletrim shivered.

He noticed Grandfather watching him.

"Ready?"

Spindletrim made a little nod. "Yes."

Ready for what? How odd he hadn't seen the shop this way before; yet this was how it had always been. But his mind had been closed to it, and now was open.

How many other things in all the world were waiting for his mind to open?

"This way."

Spindletrim *scliff-scliffed* at Grandfather's back between the glass cases, past a wardrobe with a mirror even spottier than Spindletrim's bedroom mirror. His dressing-gown brushed along cluttered shelves. A typewriter's keys begged for fingers. A cardboard box sagged with rusty horseshoes.

The grandfather clock towered against the wall, high and black, twice the height of Grandfather, smiling its silly painted smile; sixty-eight minutes past midnight.

Grandfather glanced towards the shop window. Spindletrim saw only that the blind was down.

Grandfather pulled his watch-chain free of his waistcoat. He used a key that hung on the chain to unlock the door of the grandfather clock.

The key turned and the door swung. Spindletrim leaned to see the clock's dead cog-wheel heart, but –

Grandfather *stepped inside*.

"Grandad!"

Grandfather's slim hand beckoned from the monster's gloomy body.

It was like walking into a coffin. "Pull the door shut."

Scrape! A match exploded, and Grandfather's face glowed. The glow wobbled on a candle in a candlestick. "The matches stay on this shelf," explained Grandfather. "Along with a candle or two. Look."

The candle rose and moved to where the back of the clock should have been.

Spindletrim gasped at a staircase. He frowned at the steepness and narrowness of the staircase. His heart drummed at the thought of squeezing his bruised body up that stairy tunnel –

"Come along."

Grandfather went up easily, the candlelight dropping his shadow over Spindletrim.

"Wait!" whispered Spindletrim.

"Come."

"I can't!"

"Stay."

"I can't!"

"Come." Grandfather's voice fell from amid the candleglow.

Spindletrim jammed his shoulders between the walls. He pushed, finding a step with his scliffy slipper, sniffing the smell of plaster and stone, and the waxy stench of the candle.

"It's so tight! Grandfather, I'm hurting!"

Spindletrim squealed at his bruises. The more he yowled the more crush, crush, went the walls.

So he rested, whimpering, wondering where his bravery had gone. The candlelight was a star.

Then he whimpered less, and the crushing plaster seemed to stand aside, making Spindletrim wonder if he were shrinking, but it was too dark to look, and *that* was something he wouldn't believe! Boys don't shrink! Boys are brave! And he found suddenly, he was free to shuffle up a sudden run of steps.

He was near the top, he thought, when something sighed! at his ear, jerking a scream onto his tongue. Instantly, darkness squashed him, thick as fur; but no one came because of his scream.

And he wept, but no one came because of his weeping.

"I was almost at the top!" he moaned; but no one came because of his moans.

He decided to die; and Grandfather would step on his cold hand. Grandfather would carry his dangling body into Steep Street and the bullies, on their way to steal money from the shop would stop! stunned by the silken-haired man burdened with the corpse of his grandson.

But no one came because of his self-pity, and Spindletrim found he wasn't dead. The walls had not crushed him. The sigh breathed and gurgled in the pipe inside the wall.

So Spindletrim thought of nothing, simply taking one step at a time, not caring if he trudged upwards for the rest of his life; then he tripped on the top step and fell at Grandfather's feet, startled by the light.

"There you are," said Grandfather. "I'm glad you decided to follow me. Stand up, little Spindletrim. I don't think we need the candle." Puff! and darkness rushed on them.

"Afraid?"

"No," whispered Spindletrim.

"Close your eyes."

The darkness sat like warm water. "It makes no difference, Grandad."

"Don't speak."

Spindletrim went deep inside his own head. There was nothing there.

No bullies. No Spindletrim.

Silence without words.

Silence without fear.

Silence without time.

"Enough."

"Was I asleep?"

"You were being one person, instead of two."

Something creaked. A circle of light filled a table-top.

"What do you see?" said Grandfather.

"A round table, hollow like a saucer. It's all colours." Grandfather's arm seemed cut from black paper as it reached across the table. *Creak*, and the colours sharpened. "I think . . . Oh. It's buildings! Upside down."

The picture moved jerkily until it was the right way up.

"It's Steep Street!" cried Spindletrim. "As if we were looking down from the roof!"

"We are in a camera obscura," said Grandfather.

Spindletrim didn't like the thought of being *in* anything.

"A camera obscura," explained Grandfather, "is simply a dark room."

"Oh. Is this a photograph? In colours!"

"Look again, little Spindletrim."

Spindletrim looked, for there was nothing else to see but blackness. Then he drew in a breath.

In the picture, *something moved*.

CHAPTER FOUR

"There's a man walking down the hill!"

"If you stood outside the school wall," said Grandfather from the darkness, "and held up a mirror on a stick, you would see the children in the playground?"

"Yes."

"Look. What do you see above the table?"

"A stick? Hanging down."

"A brass rod. The other end reaches the roof – attached to a mirror. I can turn the mirror with the rod." The picture blurred and swung.

"I see the whole city! Trams! People!"

"Going to work. There is a lens above us – just like in an ordinary camera – to shine the picture onto the table. I added a second lens." Grandfather crowded close to Spindletrim. "It's a bit special." A match scratched a line in the darkness, then the candle danced. "With a little adjusting . . ."

Grandfather's face peered. "Hold the rod. Steady." His fingers turned knobbles, and Spindletrim saw numbers and signs cut in the brass, like numbers on a clock and signs on a star chart.

"Grandad . . ."

"Hush, my boy. This is very delicate." Click. Whirr. Snick, snick went brass cogs under Grandfather's fingers. "Let the rod go now. I'll just focus . . . There."

"It's William Cranston! In the park! He's smaller."

"Yes," said Grandfather. "I set it for two years ago. Watch what he's doing."

"Two . . . ?"

William Cranston knelt by a flower-bed, grass around his bare knees, a jam jar in his grasp. Bees roamed. He placed the jar over a bee on a flower then guided the bee to the grass. When the bee settled on a green blade, William Cranston used the jar's rim to crush the bee.

"No!" cried Spindletrim. "Stop him, Grandad! Just because it's small!"

Grandfather reached to the brass rod. The picture jerked. A room came into focus, the square grey face of a television set flickering on Arnold Fetter. He was eating.

He finished eating and left the room. He returned with a bottle of lemonade and a paper bag. He drank from the bottle and ate biscuits until the bag was empty. He rose, then returned with a cake in a cardboard box. He ate the whole cake and finished the lemonade. Spindletrim felt ill.

The picture changed. Arnold Fetter at a football match, on the sidelines, eating.

"Why doesn't he do something!" cried Spindletrim.

"He is eating," murmured Grandfather.

Robert Snarkey stood in the playground punching a small boy, and spitting on him. The small boy's face juddered as he tried not to cry. "That's me," said Spindletrim.

"A month ago."

"Why does he do it!"

"It is in our nature to do things."

"But bullying!"

"For Robert Snarkey, it's better than doing nothing."

"And eating!"

"For Arnold Fetter, it's better than doing nothing."

"Killing bees?"

"For William Cranston," said Grandfather sadly, "it's better than doing nothing."

"I want to go downstairs," whispered Spindletrim.

Late afternoon

"Silence in court!" Spindletrim sat cross-legged at the top of his bed. The pillow balanced on his head was the judge's wig.

"The prisoner will kneel on the hardest bit of the floor. Kindly remove your hands from my bed-end. Kindly remove your hands," corrected the judge, "from the bench. Arnold

Fetter, you have been found guilty of being a fat, slobbering bully. What have you to say? Cat got your tongue? Speak up, boy! If you've something to say, say it like a man!"

The prisoner's mouth opened.

"Be quiet! The court," Spindletrim leaned towards Arnold Fetter carefully, the pillow wobbling around his ears, "knows perfectly well that you are fat. We also know that some people are naturally cuddly and quite charming with an extra stone or two; in fact, the court knows some very pretty people who are plump. Miss Melardie Brown in class 1c." Spindletrim bowed beneath his pillow to Miss Melardie Brown who had appeared in the jury, smiling prettily on the judge. "But *your* fat, Arnold Fetter is caused by eating.

"Why are you so dirty? Be quiet! Children should be seen and not heard! Five fours? Answer quickly! Miserable boy! Tell him, Miss Melardie."

"Fifteen, please sir." Smile.

"You didn't know that, did you, Fetter?"

The prisoner's mouth –

"If it takes ten men six hours to dig a ditch eight feet long, three feet wide and two-and-a-half feet deep, how long will it take five men to dig a ditch twelve feet long, four feet wide, six feet three-and-a-quarter inches deep? You don't know, do you, boy? Robert

34

Snarkey, do you know? William Cranston? I thought not! How ever are you going to get on in the world if you cannot answer important questions! Yes, Miss Melardie?"

"It takes blahr blahr blahr . . ."

"Correct. Robert Snarkey. . ." Spindletrim's head swayed sorrowfully and the pillow swung. "You were seen, Snarkey, hitting and spitting, spitting," sighed Spindletrim, "on a defenceless child, name of . . ." He regarded the clerk of the court, who was Melardie Brown.

"Spindletrim Tom." Smile.

"Spindletrim Tom. A quiet boy, interested in. . . You were seen. . ." Spindletrim remembered the table-top picture of Robert Snarkey, fists striking, face throwing spittle.

He remembered the camera obscura. His flesh hurt. He had found pink sticking-plaster on his forearm where the doctor had pushed in a needle to make him sleep. The staircase had to be a dream.

Spindletrim dipped his head, letting the pillow fall. He stepped into his slippers and went downstairs, dressing-gown flapping around pyjama'd ankles.

He stood before the grandfather clock, his pinkie nail in the clock's lock, and pulled; but it sat black and shut, dust in its grooves, smiling. Sixty-eight minutes past midnight. Getting dark. School would be out. Bullies loose.

Crash!

Spindletrim's heart jumped up and down in his chest. Shadows of William Cranston, Robert Snarkey and Arnold Fetter loomed among the junk.

"'Ere!" sneered Robert Snarkey. "Auntie's ain't doing much business! Maybe I'll buy this salt pot! Oops. Oh, look William. Look Arnold. It fell and broke. It was slippy. Somebody should clean up in 'ere!"

"Clean up!" squeaked Arnold Fetter.

"Yeah. Clean up some money," said William Cranston and swung a heavy arm without looking where the arm swung. A biscuit tin with Princess Elizabeth and Princess Margaret in a garland of flowers, tankled to the floor.

"Wot a shame," commented William Cranston. "It didn't break." He stamped on the tin and the bent Princesses smiled up.

"Yeh," breathed Arnold Fetter. "Wot a shame." He pushed crisps into his mouth as he advanced on Spindletrim. He stood, head back and poured crisp crumbs from the bag into his mouth and down his waistcoat.

Spindletrim could smell Arnold Fetter's crisp-flavoured breath. Then the bully's stomach pushed Spindletrim against the clock. "We want money!" squealed Arnold Fetter.

"Hurry up!" ordered William Cranston.

"I haven't any money!" gasped Spindletrim trying not to breathe Arnold Fetter's smell.

Arnold Fetter's sweaty palm smacked Spindletrim's forehead, cracking his skull against the clock.

Pain blinded Spindletrim, but he didn't feel like crying. Arnold Fetter hit him again. Spindletrim staggered. He was sorry for this fat smelling bully.

Then Arnold Fetter's hand slapped Spindletrim's head and the shop sloped into darkness and bottles seemed to crash against him, but he knew that *he* had crashed among the bottles. One broke its neck, and blood ran warm on his hand.

But he didn't feel like crying, and he breathed only a-little-bit-too-fast. Then Robert Snarkey's fist hit his shoulder, and the bully's face, ugly with practice, thrust down at Spindletrim. "Where's the money!"

"I haven't any money."

"The old man's stupid money!" Punch. Punch. He snatched a Toby Jug from a shelf and smashed it on the floorboards near Spindletrim's eyes, just the handle left in his fist.

"Money," demanded William Cranston, and he lifted the large jar which hadn't moved since the man brought it to the shop. "This smells like you, Arnie," laughed William Cranston, and Arnold Fetter's eyes slid miserably and he kicked Spindletrim as the bottle dropped, bursting a spray of green splinters across the floor.

A knife blade touched Spindletrim's nose; cool as his quilt. The metal shone in the dull light. Then Robert Snarkey dived at the elephant's foot, slicing the wings of the umbrellas, baring their metal bones. Arnold Fetter heaved his weight around the shop, shaking furniture, crashing piles of books. William Cranston walked, eyes shut, thrusting his arms, striking Grandfather's dusty treasures to the floor, and – it seemed to Spindletrim – feeling no pain when his wrist hit an edge of a chest of drawers.

Then the bullies left, crunching on a carpet of glass and broken china.

The umbrellas deserved sympathy for their tattered wings. The corn dolly, trampled by Arnold Fetter, lay flat as a table-mat. Books sprawled like dead seagulls.

Spindletrim breathed fast. He felt very alone. A brass candlestick smashing through the glass shelves of the display case had sent echoes into Steep Street. But no door had opened; no whistle beckoned a policeman.

Spindletrim struggled out of the mess of bottles. His breath juddered in his chest. "Grandfather!" he wept.

"I'm here, little Spindletrim," said Grandfather Tom, and he guided Spindletrim to the kitchen and bathed his head, stuck plaster on his cut hand.

"I didn't cry," said Spindletrim, "until they were gone. Then my body cried. *I* didn't."

"Very good," said Grandfather Tom. "What did they want?"

"They said you had money."

"Oh, money," smiled the old man.

"Grandad . . ."

"Yes, my boy?"

"Why wasn't I afraid?"

"Oh. Because you weren't thinking of yourself."

Next morning

Scrape, scrape, in the kitchen. Grandfather Tom, silken hair hanging at his cheeks, writing at the table. *Scrape,* went the pen. Spindletrim sighed. He hated returning to school.

Grandfather dipped the nib into the bottle of purple ink. The cork lay wet on blotting paper, staining the paper with spreading horrid blood.

"This letter," said Grandfather, "will help. You won't go to school for a day or two – " he pulled his watch into his palm, " – so if you run to the post now, the headmaster will have the letter tomorrow morning."

"Yes, Grandad," sighed Spindletrim. He wriggled into his shoes. Grandfather found a stamp in his waistcoat pocket, licked it, laid it on the envelope, thumped the King's head.

"Grandad?"

"Yes, Spindletrim?"

"Nothing." He knew school was waiting. Like a monster. It would devour him, day after day, for years.

He went through the shop, crunching in glass and china. He trudged up Steep Street. The sky, when he turned his face to the cool morning, was a bleak line above the gutters.

An early tram-car rattled along High Street, spilling sparks where wires criss-crossed overhead, clanging its bell at a butcher's boy wobbling on his fat black bicycle.

Spindletrim wandered among people hurrying to work. He saw girls giggling schoolwards; boys trailing schoolbags like dead bits of themselves, not quite fallen off. He glimpsed the headmaster's car, its chrome shining with Brasso.

He walked faster. William Cranston would be in the crowd; and Robert Snarkey slinking along; Arnold Fetter avoiding girls.

Spindletrim pushed between grown-ups, the envelope square and pale in his grasp, like a flag signalling, *I am a letter to the headmaster, complaining about bullies!*

The pillar box was a red man standing on the kerb, letting the crowds flow past. Spindletrim's friend. Spindletrim hid behind him every day.

Spindletrim ran against the pillar box.

His hand raised the envelope and the pillar box gaped.

Fingers closed around Spindletrim's wrist.

"'Ere!" sneered Robert Snarkey. "Oo you sending a letter to? Father Christmas!"

CHAPTER FIVE

"No!" cried Spindletrim. But the letter was snatched and passed to William Cranston. Spindletrim smelt Arnold Fetter's chocolatey breath on his cheek.

"It's to the headmaster," said William Cranston.

"Now," sneered Robert Snarkey, "wot would your old grandad write to the headmaster about?"

" – about," squeaked Arnold Fetter.

"It better not be about us! Got it?"

"Listen," said William Cranston. "*Dear Headmaster* – Wot a scrawl! Old Bloomsbury wouldn't let him off if he was in her class! *Dear Headmaster* – "

"He! He! He! He! Heee!" sniggered Robert Snarkey.

"He! He!" squeaked Arnold Fetter.

" – *since my letter has been stolen by Robert Snarkey* – "

"He! He! Stop larking about – "

"That's wot it says – *stolen by Robert Snarkey, and William Cranston is reading it out loud* – "

"It doesn't say that!"

"It doesn't!" squealed Arnold Fetter.

42

"See for yourself!" growled William Cranston, and the bullies snatched the letter.

"I can't make it out!" squealed Arnold Fetter.

" – *and Arnold Fetter says he can't make it out* – " read William Cranston who had snatched the letter back.

"It doesn't say that!"

"Bloomin' does!"

"Start again!" cried Robert Snarkey. "Shut up, Arnie!"

And Spindletrim, quite forgotten by the bullies, stood listening in astonishment.

> *"Dear Headmaster,*
> *Since my letter has been stolen by Robert Snarkey, and William Cranston is reading it out loud, and Arnold Fetter says he can't make it out, I will therefore address William Cranston, Robert Snarkey and Arnold Fetter.*
> *Dear William Cranston, Robert Snarkey and Arnold Fetter,*
> *I would like to remind you that you owe me three shillings and sixpence for the breakage of a jug. Further breakages are as follows:*

1 glass display case	*£2.5.8d*
1 banjo (two strings)	*8/6d*
23 picture postcards	*3/10d*

> 16 cups and 14 saucers   7/4d
> 1 straw dolly   5½d
> 5 umbrellas   14/9¼d
> 47 various glass bottles   19/-
> 1 large Arnold Fetter bottle –"

"It doesn't say that!" squealed Arnold Fetter.

"It does! And there's more! Pages of it!" William Cranston flicked through Grandfather Tom's letter. "'E says we owe him eighteen pounds, four shillings and thruppence-three-farthings! Where we gonna get that!"

"'Ere!" shrieked Robert Snarkey. "We ain't giving *him* money! *He's* giving *us* money! It's his fault! Having a stupid shop full of junk! He's *asking* people to go and smash it up!"

"'Yer," squealed Arnold Fetter.

"Shut up! Shut up! SHUT UP!" bellowed William Cranston. He shook Grandfather's letter in Robert Snarkey's face. "'Ow did he know?"

"Wot?"

"'Ow," whispered William Cranston above the rattle of a tram, "did – he – know?" He faced Robert Snarkey quietly, then tilted his glance at Arnold Fetter. "'Owdidheknow-we'dpinchhisletterandIwouldreaditandArnie-wouldsayhecouldn'tmakeitout! 'Ow –" he hissed, "– did – he – know?"

Then his eye landed on Spindletrim.

Motor cars groaned past the kerb at Spindletrim's back. The bullies glared. Spindletrim darted behind the pillar box and fled into the crowd. It was like running in an endless playground with shopping bags and briefcases to thrust against; and the bullies ran uncertainly, saw Spindletrim, less bold at pushing past men in suits, men in working clothes carrying toolbags.

He ran towards the sound of the school bell. A dash of late pupils pattered between the gateposts. Spindletrim ran among them.

He sat gasping at his desk, spots of pain where bruises objected to his running.

The teacher said, "How are you feeling, Spindletrim? You really should let people know you're being bullied. You're a silly boy. I've half a mind to punish you for not speaking up like a man . . ."

Spindletrim felt tears warm his eyes. His breath tried to escape from his chest. Why was he being threatened with punishment? The same old torture. How he hated school! And that was when he remembered he was supposed to be at home! He had come back two days early!

He was furious. He brushed tears from his eyes and stood up. The teacher blinked. Every face turned. What was timid Spindletrim up to? He could see their surprise. "I can't speak up like a man," he said.

"Spindletrim – !"

"I'm a boy! I'm a silly boy! Why should I be punished for not being a man! I'm always being punished for not being something! I'm punished for not being good at geography! I'm punished for not being good at sums! I'm punished for not being good at games!"

"How dare – !"

But Spindletrim growled. He suddenly knew there were many ways to be silly. He was silly. But the teacher was silly. There was no point, he realized, in being at school. So he ran. From the classroom –

"Spindletrim Tom! Come back here at once!"

– along the corridor. Across the playground. Into the road. Panting. No one followed. The bullies would be at their desks by now. Spindletrim walked.

He felt strong, suddenly, in his mind. It seemed that he'd been looking at his life through thick frosted glass, and the glass was shattered, letting him see. He remembered the shop, dusty, the junk unsold, and thinking his mind had opened then. It had opened again. Perhaps it would keep opening, letting him see more and more.

He stopped at the pillar box. He knew it was red, of course, but now he stood astonished at its redness; at the neatness of the white plate with black numbers. He read the numbers and the printing. He had never troubled before to pay attention. For a moment he could not think what COLLECTIONS meant. Then he understood that the postman would come – why, he had seen the postman emptying the pillar box! The postman would *collect* the letters at these times! He had never thought.

He had never thought.

Spindletrim's mind opened further. He really never had thought. About anything. Except himself.

The pillar box grinned without teeth. Spindletrim smiled back. "Thank you," he whispered, and examined a tram-car that shuffled where its rails met more rails curving into High Street. The tram was red and green.

He knew that, of course, but. . . Well. Somehow he'd never noticed. He watched the wheels; like train wheels, only smaller and without the shifting arms that join train wheels. And what a wonderful noise! Clanging and bashing, crunching, echoing under the tram-car's metal body.

He looked around for something else to notice. A doorway squashed between shops; a doorway of stone; but stone that grew into stony flowers and fruit. He gazed higher, and found among chimneys, statues of grand men. He wondered if they were new.

He strolled, staring hard at people; into

shop windows; finding in the grocer's window a block of butter as heavy as himself, glistening yellow on a square white porcelain base with BUTTER printed in black on the base's edge. A sack of lentils, the canvas top rolled open, brimming orange-pink. And two women, chatting close, one face as pale as wood in a newly-sharpened pencil, the other with cheeks crimson like fried bacon; and he remembered Melardie Brown in the art class announcing she had mixed flesh-colour; but the more flesh he saw, the more colours he discovered.

Spindletrim looked so hard at things, he didn't look where he was going. His eye took him to a new shop window. He trotted after a woman with the blackest hair and crimson lips. He found a crack in the pavement wandering wonderfully. . .

He stood before a statue in a square.

The grass in the square was green with life; and the statue rose magnificently in the still air, its chest hidden by a shield, its right arm defying the clouds with a sword.

Clouds.

Spindletrim peered at the sky. He couldn't see it. Certainly, there were no clouds. A yellow haze hung above the square. The gutters of the high buildings faded; then the top windows faded.

The morning was getting dark.

CHAPTER SIX

Fog.

Not the pearl-light fog that drifts off the sea, but fog belching from a hundred-thousand chimneys, rolling yellow down slates, spilling off gutters; burying the city, sticking to stonework, leaning its treacly weight on windows; sinking over lamp posts, swallowing their iron bodies with its descending bulk of sulphur and soot; silent against the pavement, blocking roads from cobbles to chimney tops.

Leaving you alone with your feet and your ears.

Spindletrim stamped the pavement. The sound of leather on cement vanished into brown silence.

Then the street lights flickered on, but hung dim, floating, thought Spindletrim, in a yellow ocean. And he was at the bottom of the ocean.

He heard a car, and two lamps crawled close chugging past into nothingness.

A woman's voice. "It's a real pea-souper!"

Even shop windows had faded quite away. Except the one at Spindletrim's back. A warm window crammed with brown bread and white bread, pies, cakes and stacked-up biscuits. Spindletrim remembered it was a while since breakfast.

Time to be home. He walked into gloom. He looked back. Just three or four paces away, the bakery window spread its light through the fog. He walked a few more steps and turned again. The light was gone.

He touched the wall of the buildings and walked on. Another glow appeared and he felt his way past a chemist's. He remembered looking in earlier, at the great pointed jars heavy with purple liquid.

Footsteps, as people passed invisibly, or loomed close. "Sorry, sonny!" disappearing.

Spindletrim felt his way along the building, finding the damp chill of railings in his grasp. "Oh, yes!" he said. The spikes on the railings were leaves. He had joked to himself about iron leaves on iron trees and iron apples in the fruit shop window. Then the railing became a stone column, and at the column, turned a corner. Spindletrim knew he hadn't turned a corner. At least, he thought he hadn't. He definitely hadn't.

Maybe.

Feet pattering, and boys' voices. They should be at school, thought Spindletrim. He stood close to the pillar, and the boys passed, one peering uncertainly. They dissolved like ghosts.

Spindletrim left the pillar, and scliffed like

a blind child towards the kerb. He could see his hands. He could just see the pavement at his feet. How wide was the road? A car gurgled. A single headlamp sniffed past, slower than walking. He stepped onto the road and strode swiftly, listening, tripped on the next kerb, fell against a lamp post. The light above him was the softest glow.

"Hello," called a voice. Pad, pad. "Is someone there! Are you hurt? I heard you fall."

"I'm all right, thank you," said Spindletrim.

A man appeared, as if he were stepping through a curtain. "Filthy stuff," he said. "Are you lost?"

"I'm not sure."

The man stood closer. His black coat was open at the neck showing Spindletrim a minister's white collar.

"Where do you live, my boy?"

"Steep Street, sir."

"Steep Street? That's not part of my parish, but no doubt we can find it."

"It's near High Street," said Spindletrim.

"I have just come from High Street. I'll take you back, shall I? This way. You'd better hold my hand. My goodness! No wonder it's called pea soup. Though I doubt if my wife's soup is as thick as this."

So Spindletrim followed the minister, staring at brown nothing. Occasionally seeing the floating globe of a street light. Walking into a newspaper stand, startled at the middle-aged face of a dwarf frowning up at him; listening to the minister saying they would arrive soon; he knew the way; follow him; hadn't he just been in High Street?

But the minister released Spindletrim, his hand tightening his coat collar; and a voice called words Spindletrim couldn't understand; but he knew it was the dwarf calling for customers in the fog; and for a second Spindletrim peered back.

Then he turned again. He could see no one.

"This way, my boy," said the minister faintly. "Don't worry. I'm coming."

But though Spindletrim shouted, the only answer was the news-vendor sounding like a strange fish in this strange ocean.

Silence.

Fog rolling around his bare legs.

"Eeoink!" croaked the dwarf.

Spindletrim stood still. Should he ask the way to Steep Street? He had never spoken to a dwarf.

"Eeoink!"

Did it speak English?

"Eeoink."

Spindletrim walked towards the voice. He found the little man huddled in a big jacket, a frill of papers under his arm.

"Please, sir – "

"Eeoink." A paper leapt into the dwarf's stubby hand, and pointed at Spindletrim.

"I'm lost," whispered Spindletrim.

The dwarf's mouth spread tight across his face. "D'you want a paper? Eeoink!" he projected into the fog.

"No. I live in Steep Street."

"You don't want a paper?"

"I've no money."

"Eeoink!" The big jacket turned its back. "Eeoink! Eeoink!"

Spindletrim stepped away. He bumped into a coat, and he cried out as he sat on the pavement with a bump that shook his bones.

"Sorry! Sorry!" cried a voice that poured down loudly on Spindletrim's head. "Are you hurt?"

"Oh!" gasped Spindletrim, and the coat flapped in his face, and hands like pale octopuses drifting in the ocean, clamped on his arms and lifted him.

"You should be at home!"

"I'm lost!" Spindletrim gaped up; he could scarcely see the man's head, so high was it in the fog. And the coat flapped monstrously.

"Lost?" bellowed the man. "Where does a little chap like you live? Eh?"

"Steep Street."

"Steep Street? Steep Street? Don't y'mean Level Road? I know Level Road."

"Steep Street. It's near High Street."

"Ah. I know High Street. That way. Turn right. Straight on. Can't miss it. I'd take you, but I'm not going that way – "

"Eeoink."

"Give me a paper, Sammy. Turn right, son. Straight on – "

And rather dazed, Spindletrim found a wall and perhaps turned right, but it was difficult, so difficult! to know; but his right hand brushed the stone, and straight on he walked, staring hard. Then a haze of shop windows dazzled him, and a tram clanged, a luminous leviathan swimming ponderously; and by peering, Spindletrim saw the tram was yellow and green, not red and green; so this was not High Street.

A woman heaved out from a grocer's doorway, stacked with white-strung parcels, dangling bags and a basket packed with blue-paper blocks of sugar. A smell of smoked bacon and oatmeal mingled into the taste of fog.

"Please . . ." said Spindletrim.

A small boy clung behind the shopping bags.

"I've no money!" cried the woman.

"I'm lost," said Spindletrim.

"So am I," sighed the woman, but she spoke to herself. "Where do you live?" she asked gently. "Stand still, Tommy!"

"Steep Street."

"Oh. I know it. Past Level Road."

"It's near High Street."

"Well. You're a bit away from home. Shut up, Tommy! Along here," she nodded. "Turn right at the dress shop. Past the tea room. Left at the shoe shop. Cross at the hat shop. Follow the road past the Co-op, and you're nearly there. Can't miss it, love. Tommy, get your fingers out the basket! Know where you are now? That's it. Tell your mother from me, you shouldn't be out alone. Tommy, I'll slap you! Don't walk in front. Hold my coat . . ."

Some people were kind, thought Spindletrim, but no one was going his way.

He turned right at the dress shop, staring for a moment at the dresses in the window wrapped in tissue paper to keep off the fog. Right, he turned, and the city vanished into brown rustlings of tram-cars on distant rails.

He surprised himself by approaching a glow and finding the tea room, but past the tea room, fog stood thick and still.

Spindletrim walked, fingers on walls; on a window; on nothing.

He hesitated, wandering.

Nothing to touch but cobbles. He looked at his hands to give his eyes something to focus on.

"I'm lost," he said. "I'm lost!" he called.

Listen.

A door closing.

Listen again. Hear the silence that Spindletrim heard; the silence with the beat-beat of life in your breast; with the flow of breath in your nose; the sparkle of thought behind your eyes; the thud of fear at the back of your brain.

"I'm lost!" shrilled Spindletrim. "Somebody help me!" But his voice was gulped down by the fog.

"Who can help me?" whispered Spindletrim.

He stood still, his shoes coggling on the cobbles, bending his ankles. His little legs hung down cold now from his shorts and his eyes stung and his nostrils felt gummy. One finger in his nostril came out black, and fear grew behind his brain.

"Can no one help me!" he squealed. But the fog wrapped moist arms around him, squeezing with silence. Then he remembered the silence of the camera obscura and the peace of being one Spindletrim. So he shut his eyes, and fear dissolved from the back of his head; but when he shouted at the faint blob of a window lit one storey above the pavement, still no one answered.

Laughter.

"Hello?" said Spindletrim. "Do you know the way to Steep Street? Where are you?"

Running feet.

Silence sighing around him.

"I know the way to Steep Street!" cried a voice eager with confidence, and Spindletrim turned. He turned again, cobbles slipping under his leather soles.

"Which way, please?"

"Follow!" But the voice was behind Spindletrim whichever way he faced, and he would not walk backwards; and the voice ceased.

Spindletrim wondered if it was real. He wished Grandfather would appear. He wondered if the bullies could find their way in a fog. They were so confident. Slapping, punching, tugging hair. So sure! Why were they so sure!

Then –

CHAPTER SEVEN

A match scraped. And a face with cupped hands and blue smoke twisting into the fog, strolled close.

"Lost, kid?" said the man.

"Yes."

The face grinned, and the hands descended into pockets, leaving a cigarette tilted in the mouth. The cigarette shone hot red, and the grin around it struggled to stay in place. Spindletrim decided it wasn't a real smile, but an upside-down scowl.

"I'm going your way, kid. Follow me. Come on, then."

"You don't know where I live," mumbled Spindletrim.

"Sure I do. I won't hurt you. Well? You coming? Walk beside me. Sure I know where you live. See your mother around the shops – Hey!"

Spindletrim ran.

He dodged a lamp post that rose before him.

The man followed.

Spindletrim felt fog raw in his throat. Running uphill was difficult. He began to think. *While I'm running, he can hear me. If I stop, he'll go past*.

Spindletrim stopped.

Then he walked tip-toes, following his right hand.

"I won't hurt you."

The man was panting. A red spot glared at mouth height.

"I know you're there! I see you! So c'mere! It'll be all the worse when I get you!"

Spindletrim waited. He smiled, curiously calm. He had THOUGHT. He was pleased about that.

The man shouted horridly, then his footsteps took his voice away.

Spindletrim's eyes ached; partly from the sting of dirt, partly from having nothing to look at.

He walked in a straight line and found glass at his face, black enough to show his own ghost. He stared up. The pea soup hung thick over a shop name. The pale blot of a street light hovered dismally. Spindletrim crouched, rubbing his legs to warm their bare flesh.

A voice.

Spindletrim stopped rubbing. A voice, singsong to itself, and a nun's shape grew solid a yard away. Then the light reached down and gave colour to the nun, showing Spindletrim a woman, her voice sing-songing from the huddle of a shawl around her hair.

"I'm lost," said Spindletrim. But the woman's fingers filled her ears and her eyes lay shut, and she sang, "Guide me, voices in my head. Do I need to see? Do I need to hear? Guide me . . ."

Then she dissolved.

Spindletrim wondered if sleep had crept over him. Was he dreaming this next shape, hunched, and turning every way under the lamp post? muttering, "If I'm in a fog, everyone's in a fog." It strode close, hunched still, raised a brick in its grasp, leaned back ready to smash the glass –

"Stop!" said Spindletrim, and the brick dropped as the figure scuttled into darkness.

Then merry laughter and the touch of feet going downhill, and under the light, men and women, children playing, or perched on men's shoulders. A man smiled at Spindletrim, and beckoned. "The fog doesn't matter. Just keep going down." And they pranced into thicker gloom.

Spindletrim knuckled his eyes, finding grit. He hoped the fog would blow away. He wished he was home.

Then he used his new ability: he THOUGHT.

He used his feet to walk to the lamp post, then used his hands to climb the lamp post, and clinging like a monkey, he used his eyes to see the name of the shop, because if he recognized it . . .

Brown strands of fog drifted over the shop name. Green slime cut the name leaving gold letters faint on black wood, and Spindletrim said, "Huh!" with astonishment, and slid to the road, darting on cobbles, jangling into the shop, smiling at the junk, saying, "Ha," in delight, to the grandfather clock. He blew into the Arnold Fetter bottle, twisting his nose against the smell, touched the corn dolly's cheek with a kiss of a fingertip, rattled his thumb along the crocodile's teeth –

He hesitated.

He snipped the switch and light spread thick in the foggy air. Everything was normal.

But –

Spindletrim gazed at prickles on a cactus. He stepped among bottles, plucking at the plaster on his hand; lifted an umbrella from the elephant's foot, then let it slide back with a rustle of silk.

He was hungry.

His fingers tapped a beat on the glass of a display case. *Brump*, said his fingernails.

"Oh, well," sighed Spindletrim. *Brump*. "It must be lunchtime."

Brumpity-brump.

"Or teatime."

Brump-brumpity.

"What is different?" he wondered, but though he stared ever-so-hard, and frowned ever-so-fiercely, the shop still looked normal.

"I wonder where Grandfather is."

He strolled through the curtain into the passage. He stopped and returned to the shop, the curtain swinging against his back.

"There is something different," he told himself.

Then he said, "Oh!" quite loudly.

CHAPTER EIGHT

"Grandfather!" shrieked Spindletrim. He turned, tangled suddenly in the curtain, boxed free, and fled into the passage, burst into the kitchen –

"Grandfather – !"

Oh! He had to tell Grandfather everything was back the way it was! Before the bullies smashed . . .

Spindletrim stopped, his feet slipping a little on the linoleum, one hand reaching behind him towards the door.

The man at the cooker stirred in a pot with a wooden spoon. His hair hung like silver threads on the worn collar of his shirt. His wrists ran thin from his shirt cuffs. When he turned, a smile leapt onto his face and clung there.

But he wasn't Grandfather.

Spindletrim's fingers stretched rigid. A caterpillar made of ice wriggled down his spine.

The face wearing the smile was too high towards the ceiling, because the man was too tall. The hand holding the wooden spoon clenched too tightly around the spoon's handle, choking it. And the face, though thin like Grandfather's, looked at Spindletrim through green eyes, green and thick like pea soup, rather than blue and clear like the summer sky; and above the face, the forehead rose too smoothly; Spindletrim turned, the bones of his feet pressing the floor to send him running, but the man spoke, saying – too quietly – "Little Spindletrim? What a pleasant surprise. Lost in the fog? A natural mistake to find your way to me. I do so admire your Grandfather. Please sit at my table and share my stew. Steak, y'know. Steak and tomatoes and gravy. And potatoes."

His smile crawled up to his eyes.

Spindletrim hesitated. His tummy rumbled and the man's head tipped as if asking a question.

Fog lay in the street, full of strange people, and this kitchen was so like home.

Spindletrim moved sideways as the man pointed at the table with the spoon. Gravy dripped onto the linoleum.

"Good!" cried the smile. "Excellent! I don't often eat with company. One of my regrets is that I have no grandson. Your grandfather, he has a grandson. . . Ho! Ho! But you know that. A dollop of stew. Two dollops! Dollop! dollop! on a plate. That's my plate, so it's hot. I'll get another. . ."

And he took a plate from the cupboard, and he looked so much like Grandfather that Spindletrim wondered again if a dream had sunk around him and he really was home, and the dream had changed Grandfather the silly way dreams do; then the juicy smell of stew awakened water in his mouth and he ate using a fork pushed across the table by the man; who was not Grandfather.

The man who was not Grandfather sat with Spindletrim and stew vanished into his smile, was chewed by his smile and swallowed, bumping over his Adam's apple. And he talked, saying, "Well, well, well, well, well, well, this is perfect! Little Spindletrim – that's what your grandad calls you? – little Spindletrim, eating stew at my table. Did you note the cooker? War-time? Gas? And the lino worn around its tippy-toe feet?" The smile stretched almost up to his ears and a lump of stew leapt within the cage of his teeth. "And the towel on the string? Did I get that right? And blue curtains? They are a little heavy I think, but good quality. Is there something wrong with the towel?"

"I don't understand." Spindletrim panted because he had eaten very fast. He had never tasted steak before. "I'd better go – "

"No, no, no, no, no, no. It's still foggy. And I want to know what you think of my home. The towel – ?"

"What do you mean? Are you Grandfather?"

"No, no! Oh! what a compliment! No! No!

No! No! No! No! No! No! No! Not Grandfather! Oh! Ho! Ho! Ho! Ho! Ho! Ho! Ho! Ho! Ho! Ho! Ho! Not Grandfather! but I do so admire him! I recognize his qualities! His humbleness, his quiet good manners, and always a smile!" The man smiled making his ears move back to give the smile room. "So tell me, little Spindletrim, is my kitchen – " the silver hair rustled on the man's collar as he turned his head, " – is my kitchen just like your kitchen at home? Eh?"

"Well . . ." Spindletrim remembered that the towel had split when his fingers prodded into it, but that was not important. "It's *very* like it . . ."

"Oh! Admirable! Capital! Excellent! And the shop! What did you think of the shop?"

"I'd like to go home now."

"Yes! Yes! Yes! Yes! Yes! But not yet, my boy. Your grandfather calls you my boy? Yes? Excellent! Through to the shop! This way! Ha! Ha! You really thought you were home? The curtain across the passage? It's just right? Listen!" And he opened the curtain with a rush of wooden rings on the curtain pole. *Rush!* shut. *Rush!* open. And Spindletrim realized the curtain at home ran on wooden rings on a wooden pole; though he hadn't noticed.

"It sounds the same," he said politely, wondering why the rush of a curtain mattered.

"Look around! Look around! The corn dolly's correct?" His hand snatched up the dolly, a thumb clumsy around its neck, bending the head as if it were ashamed.

"Yes."

"And the Arnold Fetter bottle?"

"Yes."

"The grandfather clock! Is it – ?"

"Well – "

The man dashed to the clock and stood too tall beside it. "Is it not right? Sixty-eight minutes past midnight?"

"Oh, yes." But the clock's smile was too wide and its eyes stared, green and thick like pea soup; but it was not worth mentioning. "May I see inside?"

The man's smile sagged. "Inside? Of course not! Inside? What does it matter what's inside?" Smile. "My dear little boy – " Spindletrim stepped back, a glass case pushing its corner into his right shoulder-blade. "What's inside doesn't matter. My goodness! you have a lot to learn! Nobody, my boy, *sees* inside! So!" And the "So!" rose, spreading across the ceiling, rattling down among jars and vases. "So! if nobody sees it – it doesn't matter! Look!" And he pounced on the umbrellas in the elephant's foot and asked questions that were so silly that Spindletrim said, Yes, to them all, though the umbrellas, he saw, were new, with walnut handles and gold ferrules; and ornaments in the glass cases still wore price tags hanging from their necks showing what the man had paid for them in Woolworth's; that the Arnold Fetter bottle shone clean on the outside though its smell hung inside, waiting for nostrils.

And Spindletrim stared where fingers pointed, and said, Yes, Yes, Yes, Yes, Yes, Yes, Yes, Yes, Yes, Yes, Yes, Yes, Yes, Yes, Yes, Yes, Yes, Yes, to keep the man's smile hanging from his ears; and the more Spindletrim looked, the more difference he saw between this shop and Grandfather's shop in Steep Street. And he sighed and gazed out at the fog, seeing darkness thicken, making the fog, it seemed, lean heavily against the windows; and the street light stared down like a strange creature hanging luminous in a brown ocean.

"I must go home," said Spindletrim.

"Yes," said the man. "I hope you enjoyed my stew. You don't have to pay for it. Oh, customers!" And Spindletrim found the curtain flapping on his face, *rush!* shutting him in the passage, wondering why he had been pushed out of sight.

"Good afternoon, gentlemen," crooned the man as the door jangled. "Do look round. Do look. . . Do look. . ."

Silence listened behind the curtain with Spindletrim.

His little fingers gathered the curtain's edge, and his eye found a gap and stared into the shop; stared wide –
at William Cranston
Robert Snarkey
and Arnold Fetter.

CHAPTER NINE

The light bulb swung. Bullies' shadows dodged among the furniture. William Cranston's shadow pressed over the man's face. Spindletrim saw that the man's shirt-front was screwed tight by William Cranston's fingers.

Arnold Fetter stood fat, head turning, eyes jumping from bottles to shelves; head tilting at the corn dolly –

"We got a question for you," said William Cranston, and the man's pea-green eyes rolled towards Spindletrim at the curtain.

"'Ere Rob – " squeaked Arnold Fetter.

"Tell us," crooned William Cranston, "'ow you wrote that letter. We'd like to know. We are int'r'st'd in things like that. Ain't we boys?"

Robert Snarkey said, "Yer," but Arnold Fetter bobbed anxiously. His head stared down at the Arnold Fetter bottle.

"'Ere, Rob . . ."

"Wot?"

"Something's different, Rob."

"Wot! Wot you on about? Will, wot's he on about?"

"Boys – " said William Cranston patiently.

"'Ere, Will – "

"*Wot is it!*" bellowed William Cranston.

"Something's different, Will!" squealed Arnold Fetter.

"I," said William Cranston, "is trying to ask this gentleman a question – "

" 'Ere!" sneered Robert Snarkey. "Something *is* different."

The bullies glowered around.

William Cranston's thick arm shot in front of Robert Snarkey as if to hold him back.

"'E's cleaned the place!" bellowed William Cranston. "Haw! Haw! Haw! Haw!"

"Heeeee!" sniggered Robert Snarkey.

"He! He! And after we smashed it up!" squeaked Arnold Fetter. "He, he, he, he, he, he, he . . ."

"Haw! Haw . . ."

"Heeeee . . ."

"Haw . . ."

"Hee."

"Haw."

The electric bulb stared at the shadows.

Arnold Fetter whispered, "Oooooh!" and reached for the door, but Robert Snarkey dived faster and clattered into the street.

William Cranston's boot kicked the door shut, cutting loose a drift of fog, stopping Arnold Fetter; releasing the man's shirt.

"How dare you attack me!" gasped the man. "I — "

Slap!

Spindletrim's cheek crinkled as the slap and William Cranston's voice came through the curtain. He knew what that slap felt like.

So he THOUGHT.

Then he ran, loud on the linoleum, hoping the two bullies would follow, and unbolted the door at the end of the passage.

Fog swallowed him. Spindletrim swam into an alley.

He heard feet behind him, and William Cranston's bellow.

Arnold Fetter squeaked, "Oo's there?"

Spindletrim laughed; the way a bully would laugh at tricking someone. So he laughed at Arnold Fetter, and Arnold Fetter's feet pounded through the fog.

"Ha! Ha!" laughed Spindletrim.

Pound.

"Ha! Ha! Ha!" Spindletrim stopped under a glowing fish in the brown ocean. He wasn't amused. He tried laughing again but the fog roughened his throat. He felt *wrong*.

"Oo's that?" squeaked Arnold Fetter loudly.

"Oo's there?" squeaked Arnold Fetter faintly. "Rob? Will? Rob? Will? Rob. . ?"

"Bong!" called a great voice, and Spindletrim jumped.

"Bong!"

"A church!"

"Bong!"

"Three o'clock."

"Bong!"

"Four o'clock." He listened. Four o'clock. School must have closed early for the bullies to have reached Grandfather's shop so soon.

Not Grandfather's shop.

Spindletrim peered gritty-eyed but couldn't see the church. He walked, and echoes came off the walls of the alley. He walked, and the echoes fell away and he found a low wall thick with railings. The railings rose into a tall gate fading upwards, standing open.

Gravel moved under Spindletrim's shoes. Weeds grew grey along the bottom of the gate. He found a wide stone seat and sat on it. His fingers touched cut-out writing, and he stood up, the flesh of his legs chilled on a gravestone.

He hurried back towards the gate, but railings hurried towards him. Tombstones leaned. He ran, watching his feet among the weeds. A lamp post beckoned and he stood under it, still in the graveyard. He walked into the smoky shadow of the church doorway and knocked, but the wood of the door stood so solid his little bones made no sound.

He called, finding the door open a gap, and squeezed inside, calling again, but his voice fell through darkness.

He began to squeeze out, when a dot of light moved across the darkness. He reached for it, then realized it was not close, but far away.

A candle.

"Hello?" said Spindletrim.

The dot stopped.

"Can I help you?" The dot hastened, vanished for a moment – as if behind a pillar – then wobbled closer bringing with it a man's face. "Hello," said the face. "Oh, it's you. You're not still lost!"

Spindletrim recognized the minister who had tried to help him in the fog. "Yes," sighed Spindletrim. "But I've had stew . . ."

"I've got tea and biscuits," offered the minister. "I'm sorry it's so dark, but it's not worth switching on the lights for myself. I know my way around."

"I'd like to go home," said Spindletrim, staring at the candle flame.

"No tea? I can easily . . ."

"I'd rather go home."

"Biscuits! Boys do like biscuits so very much! Follow me, and I'll give you some to put in your pocket. Just in case you wander the wrong way again."

Spindletrim followed the candle and the minister's black shoulder. "Watch you don't slip on Sir Morgan." The minister's foot tapped sharp on the floor. "His tombstone."

"He's buried inside the church?"

"Oh, yes, my boy. Lots of important people

get under my feet. He! He! He! This way. Oops! If I've bumped my head on the lectern eagle once, I've bumped it a thousand times! I'm sure I've got a bald spot. Ah. Here we are."

A door opened letting out a slice of light. They went into a room with choirboys draped on hooks along the wall – only, of course – Spindletrim smiled – the choirboys weren't inside their red and white clothes. And he turned, smiling to the door he'd come in and found it shut.

The minister was lighting a gas ring, scraping a kettle onto the ring, patting the kettle's head as if it were a pet dog. "I know you want to be on your way but I do love a cup of tea, and if you've been lost all day another few minutes won't matter. Biscuits. Now where did the boys put the biscuits? In their tummies. Ha! Ha! But – here we are." He opened a big square tin with McFarlane Lang on the sides. "No chocolate ones left I'm afraid. I do love a chocolate biscuit." The minister beamed on Spindletrim and asked his name.

Spindletrim said, "Spindletrim," and examined the minister's face above his white collar; a kind face, a little like Grandfather's, but plumpish; and his body, inside a black suit, seemed thin, but his waistcoat erupted forward over a large stomach; and a gold watch-chain glittered, thicker than Grandfather's.

"I'd like to go home," said Spindletrim.

"Tea will warm you up. I'm sorry I can't offer you anything more. Have a biscuit. Put some in your pocket. You had stew? I love stew. A nice leg of mutton. A shoulder of ham. Sheep's brains. Have you ever tried sheep's brains? And pork belly. Oh! I'm getting quite hungry. Hehehehehehe!" he giggled. "But there's no oven here to cook meat. Oh, how hungry I am!"

It seemed to Spindletrim that the minister glanced at the empty clothes of the choirboys, and he stared in horror at the minister's strong teeth. How big his mouth was when he laughed. And how his waistcoat wobbled, flashing threads of light from the watch-chain. Spindletrim bumped his cup down and stood up.

"Please, sir, I want to go home."

"Certainly, my boy. Quite right, quite right!"

"Bong!"

It seemed to Spindletrim, that the clock's voice shook the ceiling and the choirboys trembled on their hooks.

"Oh!" cried the minister, smiling a strong white smile. "Hold on! I'll show you the way. But something to do first! Come along – "

"Please, sir — "

The minister snatched open a door and

switched off the light. He clicked on another light in a passage that sloped down, and Spindletrim, with darkness at his back, followed.

"Yes!" cried the minister. "Something to do! Liver! Liver in blood! And devilled kidneys. Oh! Devilled kidneys and bacon and sausages and black pudding – "

"Please – " Spindletrim glanced back at the empty choirboys. They hung in shadow, watching him descend with the minister.

Steps took the minister down, and a switch spread light in a large low room with an arch of stone supporting the roof and fat pipes worming around the walls disappearing head first into a huge metal container. The room was warm. Spindletrim reached for a worm.

"Careful!" cried the minister. "It's hot. Central heating for the church, y'know. Got to stoke the boiler!" And he grinned and used a shovel to knock open a little iron door. Inside, flames wobbled on red hot coal.

"Coke! Spindletrim!" cried the minister, and rushed the shovel into a coke heap and heaved the shovelful into the furnace. Flames burst higher. Spindletrim stared. It was a very deep oven.

"Did you cook the choirboys in there?"

"Cook – ?" The minister's jolly gaze hung over Spindletrim. "Cook – ? Ha! Cook the – ? Ha! Ha! Ha! Cook the choirboys? Haaaaaaaa!

Ha! Ha!"

Spindletrim stepped back from under the minister's teeth, and flames leapt sending a red glow up the minister's black suit, red glitters on his watch-chain, fire and shadow on his opened face.

"Ha! Ha! Ha! Ha!" The shovel swung scraping into the coke.

"Ha! Ha! Ha!" Flames danced a wild dance.

"Ha! Ha! Ha!"

Spindletrim backed into the passage.

Scrape went the shovel. "Ha! Ha! Ha! Ha! Ha!"

Spindletrim fled up the sloping floor.

"Ha! Ha! Don't go! Ha! Ha! I won't eat you! You'll get lost again! Ha! Ha! Ha! Ha! Liver in trousers! Ha! Ha! Boys' brains and brussels sprouts! Ha! Ha! Ha! Ha! Ha!"

Spindletrim rushed past the dead choirboys and flung open the shut door into the church.

"Roast belly of boy!" shrieked from below.

Spindletrim ran in the blackness following the ends of the pews with his hand.

"Minced Spindletrim!" rose faintly behind him.

His memory took him to the gap in the great door; he squeezed free and plopped into the fog. A stone angel smiled as he fled past. Onto the pavement. Something was coming.

CHAPTER TEN

Spindletrim remembered escaping from the man with the upside-down scowl by standing still. He stood still, the sooty taste of fog on his tongue, clinging to the graveyard railing; listening.

No sound came from the church.

But out in the fog rolled a mumbling and shuffling; much too much mumbling for just one person; too, too much shuffling for only one pair of feet, but nearer it sounded, looming beneath a street light, a monster filling the pavement with its many legs and squat body.

Spindletrim pressed back against the railing. He stepped his heel onto the railing's wall and raised himself onto the wall; perhaps in the fog the monster would mumble past without noticing.

But it did notice, and its long hair released giggles, and faces peered up out of the hair.

"It's that Spindletrim!" giggled a face.

"He ran out of Bonzo Ferguson's class this morning!"

"He looks scared."

"He always looks scared! His grandad beats him!"

The monster broke up into girls, and a

round pretty face said, "Why are you hanging onto the railing?"

Spindletrim shrugged, and his little heart danced. It was Melardie Brown. He lowered himself to the pavement. "I'm lost," he said.

"Up a railing?" squealed a thin face.

Tinkles of giggles.

"We're lost too."

"I'm not!"

"It's that way!"

"Well, Susan said it's this way!"

"It isn't!"

"It is!"

"T'isn't!"

"T'is!"

"Be quiet!" said Melardie. "Is this a church?" she asked Spindletrim.

"Yes. But the minister was going to eat me. I ran out here."

"Eat you!"

"Eat a sparrow!"

"His little legs are as thin as the railings!"

Tinkle, tinkle in the fog.

"He's got an oven!" cried Spindletrim. "With red hot coal! He was going to put me in it! He kept saying how hungry he was! And talking about boys' brains! He was going to mince me!"

"Don't be horrid!"

"Boys don't have brains!"

"It's what he said."

"He didn't really?"

"Yes. I think he ate the choirboys. All their clothes are hanging on hooks."

The faces looked at each other uneasily.

"It's true," said Spindletrim, interested in the effect his words had. Though it perhaps wasn't quite true.

"Let's go."

"I want to see the name of the church," said Melardie Brown. "Then we'll know where we are."

"You look!" cried the thin face and turned pushing, and the monster moved, slowly, getting its stride, faster.

"Come on!" said Melardie, and she grabbed Spindletrim and they ran after the monster.

Their feet clattered between buildings. Giggles in the fog, until " 'Ere!" snapped along the pavement. "Oo's that!" cracked the swirling air, and they stopped, faces among the hair, Spindletrim wishing he could see over the girls.

"It's that Snarkey!" cried Melardie Brown, and Spindletrim's heart stood on its head, but he squeezed fear back from his lips, and pushed among the girls towards Robert Snarkey's voice.

He knew the bully was lost.

Robert Snarkey's thin body stepped sideways from the fog. "Oo's that?"

"It's me," said Spindletrim.

"And us," said Melardie.

Robert Snarkey's sneer bent his nose. He came close. His eyes, saw Spindletrim, were green, like something you'd blow into your handkerchief.

"Are you lost?" asked Spindletrim, wondering if the monster of girls was making him brave.

"Naw. Bet you are. Stupid."

"We might be," admitted Spindletrim, because being lost suddenly didn't matter. He had company; and they would find the way to Steep Street eventually.

"Which way you lot going, then?"

"That way."

"Let's go!" whispered thin-faced Susan. "We don't want him!"

"He's horrible!"

"He does things in the mirror in the cloakroom!"

"Nasty bully!"

"*Oo's a bully!*" Robert Snarkey's arm thrust past Spindletrim and someone squealed.

Without the least thought of running, Spindletrim's shoe came off the pavement toe-first into the bully's shin.

He clenched his fist until it felt like a stone, then drove it against the bully's ribs.

He still had no thought of running.

He kicked Robert Snarkey's shin again.

A school satchel swung from behind him

and battered the bully's head. Shrill cries, and biting sentences splintered the fog.

Robert Snarkey shouted and backed off, then he charged, his face bitter, fists knuckled for hurting.

Spindletrim punched again.

But the bully's punch was quicker and burst like an explosion on Spindletrim's cheek. The girls' feet ran away on the pavement; scattered on the road.

"Leave him alone!" shrilled a voice which might have been Melardie's.

A rough boot scraped the back of Spindletrim's legs and hooked his feet forward. He dropped hard back on the pavement, a yell bumped from his lungs.

Voices pierced the fog, Melardie screaming words. The scattered feet returned, and Robert Snarkey, saw Spindletrim as the explosion faded from his cheek, thrust his arm up against flailing satchels and danced retreating, from brave little shoes.

But the bully's strength was too much and the girls fell away, and Spindletrim rose, heart beating almost happily; pain explored his cheek.

But he never thought of running.

Then a voice said, "Here's the other one!" And heads stared, and Robert Snarkey sneered, as out of the haze, came the round shape of Arnold Fetter.

Then to Spindletrim's amazement, Melardie Brown ran towards the new bully, caught his hand –

"'Ere!"

– dragged him forward.

"You're bigger than him!" she yelled. "Send him away!"

"'Ere, Rob – !"

"Go on!" screamed Melardie getting behind Arnold Fetter and pushing. "Make him leave us alone! We didn't invite him!"

"'Ere – "

"Little Spindletrim stood up to him."

"Eh?"

"But he's not strong enough – " She pushed the bully's fat back.

"'E's my mate – "

"Some mate! Hitting people! Did he ever buy you a bag of crisps?"

"Course not – "

"Or help you with your homework!"

"Course he don't – "

"Or tell you secrets!"

"'Ere. . . You never told me no secrets, Rob."

"*Sharrup!*" screamed Robert Snarkey; and Melardie stood beside Arnold Fetter; the girls and Spindletrim stood, a monster on many legs; saying nothing.

"Sharrup! Sharrup!" Robert Snarkey strode forward but no one moved, no one even

For a moment Spindletrim remembered the choirboys, but here the bodies wore no clothes, and swung heavier than people on their hooks; chains stretched up from the hooks to pulleys; the hooks pierced the bodies, letting red drips fall on the cobbles, pink water running into drains.

"It's the slaughterhouse," said Arnold Fetter. "My dad's the foreman." So they piled through the doorway, avoiding the meat, so pink, so white with fat, swaying so massively a nudge from one could knock you over.

Fog lay under the bright lights, and men wearing rubber aprons, brick-brown aprons tight around their chests, trailing like skirts above their boots; and a fat man screwed off a tap and the splashing ceased, and the hose lay snake-like, wriggling as it dribbled water from its brass mouth.

"'Ere, Dad!" Arnold Fetter approached the man, and the man looked in surprise, and his big face had surprise spreading over it seeing girls and Spindletrim.

"'Ere!" said the man. "Where's these two bullies you hang around with? Wot are these kids doing here?"

"Lost in the fog," squeaked Arnold Fetter. "But I know the way now. Can we go through the big door, Dad? Can I show them round?"

"Show them round? Show them round?

Nobody in their right mind wants shown round 'ere. Look, son, 'ere's two bob. Some of these kids is famished. The chip shop's open . . ."

From a far place, squeals and moos rose in fear, and occasionally a horrid thud like a gun going off inside a bag. Spindletrim stared down the long rows of bodies and breathed the smell of blood and terror; he remembered the stew he had eaten. Steak, with potatoes and tomatoes, and he used his new power of THINKING, and wondered if all this jangling of chains, all this piercing of hooks through flesh, this stench – was it worth a plate of stew?

Someone shrieked and the girls fled from a giant metal bin, so Spindletrim stood by the bin but it was too high to see into, and stained brown and red; then Arnold Fetter swept down on him and lifted him, so that he saw inside the bin; and from the bin dozens of eyes stared from dozens of heads, hairy cows' heads, a bull's head as big as Spindletrim's desk in school, with a curly fringe like Melardie's; and pigs' heads, pink and bristly with great snouts and blood-black nostrils, and sheep's heads, woolly as knitted bonnets, gazing into eternity.

"Where are their horns?" asked Spindletrim. Arnold Fetter took him to peer into another bin, but he turned his face away; horns and hooves crammed high, and such a smell . . .

Arnold Fetter said, "We got to eat. Fish and chips all right? Come on. Come on you lot!" And Spindletrim followed him towards a great open door at the far end of the slaughterhouse, and the girls gathered close, sniggering a little, perhaps whimpering.

Then they breathed fog, Spindletrim pausing to spit out the flavour of blood. Someone said, "Where's that Susan?" He glanced back at the meat hanging in the slaughterhouse.

Susan, her mouth wide open and her eyes gaping at the roof-full of lights, was swaying slightly, and dangling from one of the steel hooks.

CHAPTER TWELVE

Under Susan's dangling shoes, square little rivers ran pink among the cobbles; shrieks in the street; men stood, like surgeons in the foggy-bright slaughterhouse, with their toe-tipping aprons and bloodied arms; shouting. Arnold Fetter's father ran, a knife clattering from his hand, then as he reached to the hanging child, Melardie strode forward screaming, "Come down! Come down, you lunatic!" and Susan's eyes swivelled, and her mouth shrank to its normal gape. Mr Fetter's great hands enclosed her waist; she let go the hook and he lowered her to the cobbles.

"'Ere!" he gasped.

Melardie ran and thumped Susan. "*What were you doing!*" she howled. Thump. "*What were you thinking about!*" Thump!

"Now then – " said Mr Fetter.

"That hurt!"

The girls closed around Melardie, then turned their backs on Susan.

"I wanted to know what it was like being dead."

Mr Fetter dug behind his apron. "'Ere's another two bob," he gasped. "Pickled onions, eh?"

"Pickled onions!" announced Arnold Fetter. "Fish and chips! Oo's 'ungry then? You coming, you lot?"

"We're coming," said Spindletrim, and he led Susan; and the backs broke open letting him and Susan into the monster; Melardie sniffling, Arnold Fetter straining for the chip shop.

From the great doorway of the slaughterhouse, the surgeons gazed, bodies hanging bright behind them; Susan's hook swinging a little on its chain.

"Thank you!" called Spindletrim.

"Thank you," sprinkled from the girls.

The fat man raised his hand.

"Yer," squeaked Arnold Fetter. "Thanks, Dad. Chip shop's this way." And he swaggered happily, leading the girls and Spindletrim around a corner.

Melardie's voice jabbed at Susan.

Spindletrim walked cheerfully-nervous among the girls. His mind opened again, like a door eased to let in light, for Arnold Fetter was no longer a bully, but an adult-sized bulk leading him home. Spindletrim tried to think of Robert Snarkey and William Cranston as adults, but he could not see them talking sensibly or helping anyone.

Then vinegar spiced the taste of fog, and the monster of girls swept Spindletrim into the thick light of the chip shop.

They huddled hot-handed, eating, reluctant to leave the shop's warmth, giggling over slippy pickled onions, Susan forgiven because she could push a whole onion into her mouth and close her lips; though her eyes watered.

Then on the pavement they fingered the vinegary inside corners of their chip bags, crushed the bags, some pushed into the wire bin on a lamp post, others dropped, Arnold Fetter footballing his along the pavement, then sheepishly returning when no one joined in.

Behind him, out of the fog, hurried a child; running into the glow of the shop, a coin glinting in her fingers, hesitating on seeing Arnold Fetter, coming close on seeing the girls.

"'Ere," said Arnold Fetter, "She's got a green uniform."

"It's Betty," said Melardie. "Are you lost?"

Arnold Fetter prodded the child's shoulder.

She pushed his finger away. "Hello, Melardie." Prod. "Stop it." Push his finger.

"She's got a green uniform."

"Oh, leave her alone!" said Melardie.

"But she's – "

"We know," groaned Susan. "She's got a green uniform! So what? Leave her be! You're not with Snarkey and Cranston now!"

"Yeh, but – "

Betty bounced her schoolbag on her back.

"We didn't get out early. Did you?"

Nods and voices.

"Have you had chips? Wait for me. I followed the smell. Don't go without me!"

She went into the chip shop. Spindletrim waited with the girls. Arnold Fetter waited. Swaggering. Embarrassed, saw Spindletrim, at having his bullying taken away. Then Melardie asked him to lead them home, because he knew the way from the slaughterhouse; and Spindletrim walked at the edge of the monster. Arnold Fetter sailing in front like a strange trunk raised to feel the fog; Betty and Melardie chatting; Susan scowling around, saying, "Melardie! Melardie!"

"What?"

"Nothing."

Chat between Betty and Melardie. The monster grew thinner and longer behind its Arnold Fetter trunk.

Two boys, also in Grammar School green, appeared beside Spindletrim, smiling a little, talking quietly.

The trunk stopped and the monster gathered fat, behind.

"Yer. This way," said Arnold Fetter; around the cold stone shoulder of a tenement. Spindletrim felt a windowsill, and on moist dark glass, wrote Melardie's name. Then he hurried to catch up, walking beside a girl he hadn't noticed before. There seemed to be a lot of the monster now, and more uniforms, and the chattering was loud, with steel shrieks of laughter.

Under the ocean-glow of a street light, they met another monster, coughing, waving arms, some green, some brown, dull in the fog; the new monster folded into the first; Melardie's voice rose in welcome; laughter; "Good old Arnie!"

They left the light and fumbled cold-legged through invisible streets. "Where are we now, Arnie?"

"I must pull up my stockings."

"Is that a shop?"

"There's grass here."

"I think that's a statue."

"We're in the square!" cried Spindletrim. "I was here this morning!" He stared at the shop window which had been piled with bread and biscuits, but its round stands stood bare, with odd buns and crumbs on paper doilies; then he pushed towards Melardie, and said, "That way!"

Arnold Fetter plodded, past the chemist's with its pointed jars of purple liquid; then damp railings with iron leaves on top for spikes. "Where now?" asked Melardie when they touched the stone column at the corner.

"I crossed the road," said Spindletrim. The monster spread along the kerb. "Then I got lost."

Melardie groaned.

"I ain't lost," said Arnold Fetter.

"Cross the road!" ordered Melardie, and legs surged.

But Susan cried, "She doesn't know – "

"Watch for cars," said Melardie, and the monster followed her to the far kerb, gathering under the lamp post.

Round school hats and boys' caps moved among the bare heads of the original monster. Faces receded into the fog. Arnold Fetter, Melardie and Betty, Susan and Spindledrim stood squashed beneath the light.

"'Ere, this way."

"Show us," said Melardie. "Come on!" she yelled, and Arnold Fetter became the trunk with the huge leggity creature mumbling behind him; feet applauding on the pavement; the heads bobbing past a lit window where a man paused as he mended shoes, staring out.

The flow of the monster through the fog, troubled Spindletrim. He stared back as feet beat, like bullies feet in the playground. Green uniforms strode together, swerving. "Don't push!" Brown uniforms reached for each other, linked arms and marched.

Spindletrim clung to Melardie's cuff.

He remembered the tiny Spindletrim at the edge of his mind, and felt that *he* sat now, at the edge of the monster – watching.

A great glow waiting in the fog; high as a house. The glow hardened into a tram-car as Spindletrim was swept nearer. A few people inside, peered against the glass, one man's hand bidding them away; but Arnold Fetter swaggered onto the tram's platform.

"We're stopped," said the conductor. "The fog – Hey, you can't all come on! Come on, get off. Come on!"

The monster flowed in one end of the tram and out the other.

The Arnold Fetter trunk raised its arms like a snail raising its horns, feeling the fog. Spindletrim forgot the tram-car as feet strode along pavements. Fog wisped over cobbles; it rolled along gutters.

Then light blazed from great square windows. The snail marched into the light, towards a Woolworth's door.

"We're in High Street!" said Melardie.

"Good old Arnie!" cried a voice behind Spindletrim.

"Good old Susan," said Susan; she said "Susan!" at Betty.

"Susan?" said Betty above the voices of the monster.

"Susan!" said a brown uniform.

"Arnie!" said green uniforms. "Arnie!" they chanted.

Spindletrim tugged Melardie's cuff. "Arnie!" said Melardie marching onward.

"Arnie! Arnie!"

Susan's thin face directed her voice back over the monster's body. "Susan!" she shouted. "Su*san!*" She headed for another door into Woolworth's, her little fist raised; and the monster split, part following the snail, part following the fist.

Spindletrim clung to Melardie as he was pushed through Woolworth's, for Melardie's voice was part of the monster's voice; and behind the counters, assistants gaped or shooed away hands that strayed among the Pencils 2d each, and Rubbers 1½d each, Elastic Bands 6d a packet, Dolly Mixtures 3d qtr, Pins 9d, String 1/3d, Fancy Jugs 3/6d, Glass Jugs 2/-, Drawing Books 9d and 1/9d, Sewing Kit 1/11d, Jotters 6d, Science Note Book 2/3d, Pens 4d, Face Powder 9d, Tumblers 4d, 6d and 1/1d, Blue-black Ink 6d.

The two monsters pushed tentacles around the shop's counters. Adult voices chirped fearfully; then the snail thrust towards a door, and into the street the monsters poured, gathering in the soft light, hesitating as a breeze pushed the fog into strands.

Street lights appeared bright on iron lamp posts dotting into the city's distance. Uniforms clutched their hats and ran as Woolworth ladies came out reaching for the scruffs of necks and shouting, "Thieves!"

"Melardie!" gasped Spindletrim. "You've

got a comb in your hand!"

Melardie stared at the comb. "Oh!" she gasped. She dropped the comb. "Run! This way!" Under a reaching arm, bumping against Betty who was staring horrified at a sparkly brooch.

"Run!" hissed Melardie, and they ran, clattering down the nearest side street.

They left the shouting.

Uniforms disappeared around corners.

"I didn't mean to take the comb," said Melardie.

"No," said Spindletrim.

"I have to go home." She grasped Betty's hand.

"Yes," said Spindletrim.

"You really stood up to Snarkey," said Melardie. "I didn't know you were that brave." She hurried away with Betty.

Her hand wiggled at Spindletrim, and he took her smile to Steep Steet.

Lamp posts shone on cobbles. The whisper of Spindletrim's shoes rose to the pale dark crack of sky that wandered between the gutters.

He jangled into the shop and stood under the electric light. A floor brush leaned its elbow on the counter. Broken china was pushed into a heap. A sack sagged, peeping with broken umbrellas, and the flattened corn dolly.

The hands of the grandfather clock pointed at eight minutes past one.

From behind the curtain – down the passage from the kitchen – came a sneer.

It was Robert Snarkey's.

CHAPTER THIRTEEN

"I 'erd the door jangle!" sneered Robert Snarkey.

Spindletrim thrust! aside the curtain.

"I 'erd the curtain – " said William Cranston.

Spindletrim battered into the kitchen.

Grandfather Tom sat in his rocking-chair. His face was white like egg white, and his cheek red as bacon where William Cranston's palm had struck.

Bits of Grandfather's buttery pipe lay on the linoleum.

"Grandad!" growled Spindletrim. The growl shrank his hands into fists. He jumped at William Cranston, but before he could use the fists, William Cranston pushed him against Snarkey.

Spindletrim gave the fists to Snarkey's stomach.

Snarkey's face sucked air.

Spindletrim lunged again at Cranston, but the bully threw him against the cooker. Pain – like a thousand mattress springs – dug under Spindletrim's shoulder-blade. The linoleum chilled his legs.

Robert Snarkey rose over him, sucking. Spindletrim stared up. Was that a *hoot* in

Snarkey's voice? A knife trembled in the bully's hand.

"'Ere!" said William Cranston. "Leave that out!"

The blade leapt thin at Spindletrim.

Grandfather's voice!

Robert Snarkey's eyes really were snotty green, thought Spindletrim; and he realized that the bully – like Grandfather – was one person. Grandfather was one person because he had turned all the bad things out of himself; Snarkey was one person because he had turned all the good things out of himself.

William Cranston's hands swept Snarkey aside. The knife bounced under the cooker.

Snarkey scrabbled after the knife, but William Cranston's thick fingers spun him on the floor. Snarkey kicked, and blood ran onto William Cranston's socks. William Cranston's fist released ketchup from Snarkey's nose.

Spindletrim stood with Grandfather.

Steel-tipped boots skidded on blood.

Bone struck flesh.

Gasps fled around the kitchen like terrified ghosts.

"Stop it!" whispered Spindletrim. "STOP IT!"

The bullies panted on the linoleum, Snarkey *hooting*.

"The only valuable thing," said Grandfather shakily, "is upstairs. Go into the shop.

I will show you."

They led the bullies to the grandfather clock, and unlocked the clock; scraped a match. Grandfather's fingers stood the match's flame on a candle.

The stair wobbled upwards in the candle-light.

The smell of wax mingled with the ancient taste of plaster.

"It's a trick!" shrieked Robert Snarkey. "*Hoot!* Glub! There ain't nothing up there!"

"It's too narrow," said William Cranston, moving his man-sized shoulders.

"We'll show you," said Grandfather. He went up easily, and Spindletrim walked at his side. Spindletrim's fingers tipped the mouldy stone.

"'Ow'd they do that?" shrieked Robert Snarkey. "It's too narrow!"

"I ain't going to try," said William Cranston.

"Oo cares! *Oo cares!*"

Spindletrim looked down the staircase. Light from the shop spilled around Snarkey. William Cranston loomed at Snarkey's back, saying, "I ain't going to try. I ain't – "

"'E's got money!" glubbed Snarkey. "I'm *going up!*" and the thin bully put his foot on the bottom step and behaved very curiously.

From where Spindletrim stood, far up the staircase, he could see clearly that the walls were wider than Snarkey's shoulders – but the bully squeezed, *squeeeeezed*, as if the walls squashed tight.

"Grandad?"

"Yes, my boy?" descended over him.

"The staircase isn't really narrow. Why is he squeezing?"

"His mind is narrow."

Spindletrim let this thought float in his head.

"When *I* was squeezing," said Spindletrim, "the staircase *really was* narrow."

"Was it?" breathed Grandfather.

Spindletrim gazed down at the struggling bully.

"The walls don't look as if they could move."

"No."

Spindletrim turned and faced up to Grandfather's candleglow. "Will Robert Snarkey go on struggling? Until he gets up?"

"He cannot get up by struggling. You know that."

"What will he do?"

"I expect he will struggle. All through his life. Would you like to see?"

Spindletrim ascended until he stood with Grandfather in the camera obscura.

Grandfather blew the flame off the candle. "Would you like to see?" he said again in the darkness.

"I don't know what you mean, Grandad."

"Would you like to see Robert Snarkey's future?"

Grandfather's voice turned away from Spindletrim and something creaked bringing the picture to life on the saucer-topped table. Lights shone in Steep Street. The picture jerked and the whole city sparkled.

"Hold the brass rod, my boy, and I'll just adjust – "

"Grandad?"

"Mm?"

"Is that how you wrote the letter to the bullies? Did the camera obscura show you what they would do?"

"That's right." Grandfather's black-paper arms paused above the table. He seemed to be waiting for Spindletrim to speak.

Spindletrim thought of everything he had learned in the last day or two. His mind had opened more and more. He wondered if seeing the future would really be useful. It was difficult enough understanding the present. A tiny tram-car went sparking across the table.

"I'm very hungry," he said gently.

"Ah."

"Can we get past Snarkey on the stair?"

"Switch it off, shall we?"

"Yes, please."

The picture vanished into blackness. "There's plenty of room to get past Snarkey," said Grandfather. "I seem to have left the

104

matches in the clock. I can't light the candle."

"It's all right," said Spindletrim, thinking of the glow around Snarkey's back. "There's plenty of light where we're going."

"Of course there is," said Grandfather. Spindletrim heard a smile in his voice. "There is always light when our eyes are open. A cup of tea now, I think. And bread with lemon curd. Will you be ready to go to school tomorrow? Bruises better, eh? That is excellent. You're not expecting trouble from young Fetter? And if you treat your teachers gently. . ."

Spindletrim held Grandad's hand, and with a smile in his heart to match the smile on his lips, he stepped with Grandad towards the light.

A GHOST WAITING

Hugh Scott

"The pale thing rose into the torchlight. It flapped towards Andrew and Rosie…"

It begins for Rosie and Andrew one stormy afternoon, about a year after the death of their brother James, in the gloom of their father's churchyard. A white rushing thing, a split gravestone, a sense of something lurking in the shadows… It isn't really the start, though, but the final chapter of a story begun centuries before by a scheming cleric – and continued now by a reckless teenage boy. And before the terror ends, someone must perish…

"Horror and good writing don't often go hand in hand – Scott is a master of the genre." *The Sunday Telegraph*

A BOX OF TRICKS

Hugh Scott

"Simon Welkin! Come! We would converse with thee!"

Every summer, John and Maggie are packed off to stay with their Aunt Nell and Great-grandfather Harris in the country. But this year they get an explosive surprise, when Great-grandfather decides to waken the dead!

"Hugh Scott is at his best, stretching and exciting the imagination, producing glittering effects... Eerie and occasionally terrifying, beautifully evoking dark and light... The tension mounts to make the pulse race." *Susan Hill, The Sunday Times*

"Horror-hungry 10-year-olds will love it." *The Sunday Telegraph*

"A book which will be read time and again – a captivating ghost story which could well become a classic." *Time Out*

THE HAUNTED SAND

Hugh Scott

"Murder, Frisby! Murder on the beach!"

There's something creepy in the churchyard. There's something deathly down on the sand. Darren feels it, Frisby hears it, George thinks it's a bit of a laugh. But there's nothing funny about murder…

"Intriguing ingredients abound: a haunted church; fearful chases; ghostly weeping; skulls; bronze helmets; gems and The Black Death… Rendellesque subtleties of storyline build to an unforeseen climax."
The Times Educational Supplement

THE GARGOYLE

Hugh Scott

"No! No! No! You don't understand! The fear will kill you!"

On first sight, the new Scottish home of Professor Kent and his family seems quite idyllic. But there's a chill about the place that's not simply due to snow – an atmosphere of menace that young Marion, with her psychic powers, quickly senses. It seems to have something to do with the mysterious German and a boy called Callum who live in the nearby castle. Before long, Marion and her father find themselves in a tense battle of wits and wills – a life and death struggle that brings them face to face with the terrifying gargoyle…

"Followers of Hugh Scott will relish the mannered deliberation with which menace builds up in The Gargoyle."
The Independent

"The kind of book that once you start you've got to finish. You can't possibly put it down for another sitting. It moves at a pretty cracking pace."
BBC Radio's Treasure Islands

WHY WEEPS THE BROGAN?

Hugh Scott

WED. 4 YEARS 81 DAYS FROM HOSTILITIES …
so reads the date on the clock in central
hall. For Saxon and Gilbert, though, it's
just another day in their ritualized indoor
existence. Saxon bakes, Gilbert brushes,
together they visit the Irradiated Food
Store, guarding against spiders. Among
the dusty display cases, however, a far
more disturbing creature moves… But
what *is* the Brogan? And why does it
weep?

"Deftly evoked, the narrative is cleverly
constructed, and there is no denying the
nightmarish power of the story. There is a
true shock ending." *The Listener*

"A very compelling and very interesting
book." *Jill Paton Walsh, The Times
Educational Supplement*

A Whitbread Novel award-winner
Shortlisted for the McVitie's Prize

MORE WALKER PAPERBACKS
For You to Enjoy